Do questions 1 to 4 (
for Learning 1

/, the
search
tor

MW01517612

File   Edit   View   Go   Favorites   Tools   Window   Help

Back   Forward   Stop   Refresh   Home   Autofill   Print   Mail

Address: @ http://www.thegreatcanadianadventurecontest1.html

The Great Canadian Adventure® Contest

français | help | search | a

Prepare a project on the government of Canada and the special symbols Canada has.

Canada has three levels of government. They are federal, provincial and territorial, and local. Each does different things for the people of Canada. Start by doing research to find out about Canada's federal government and the special symbols Canada has. Use non-fiction and reference books such as this book, encyclopedias, and the internet to find this information.

1

GOVERNMENT

The people in a country, province, territory, or community who make and carry out the laws.

Ms. Rose spoke to the class on what they would be learning about government. "Government is one of the topics you are to research for The Great Canadian Adventure Contest." She pointed to the definition on the whiteboard as she said, "The word *government* means the people in a country, province, territory, or community who make and carry out the laws.

"In your family, your parents make and carry out rules and look after any disputes that occur among family members. Teachers and principals also make rules for all the students and make sure they are carried out. As you read about government, use the word *laws* instead of the word *rules*.

"Canada has three levels of government. Canada has one federal government, ten provincial governments and three territorial governments, and hundreds of local governments. The federal government makes laws for all the people of Canada. The government of each province makes laws for the people living there. The mayor and city council make laws for all the people living in their community. Governments also make sure the laws are carried out. They settle any disputes and provide helpful services for the people," concluded Ms. Rose.

CHART LEGEND

- National Powers
- Provincial and Territorial Powers
- Local Powers

1	Federal Government	**Level 1**
10	Provincial Governments	**Level 2**
3	Territorial Governments	
100s	of Local (Community) Governments	**Level 3**

This chart shows the three levels of government in Canada.

This map shows two levels of government: level 1, federal government (the government for all of Canada) and level 2, provincial government (for the ten provinces and three territories).

3

Research Topic

Prepare a project on the government of Canada and the special symbols Canada has.

Tilly continued the lesson. "In an earlier social studies class, I explained how research should be carried out in an organized way. If you are not organized, it will take you longer to find the information. You might not even find the information at all. Please turn to the back cover of this book and read the three steps of research."

Change Research Topic into Questions

"Today, we will be focusing on Step 1, Gathering Research," continued Tilly. "Sophie, will you tell the class what we should do first?"

"Before starting to look up information, we should change the research topics into questions," replied Sophie.

If you can't remember the first step of doing research, see Tools for Learning 3.

Tilly asked the class what questions they had about the federal government. She wrote them on a large chart.

We want to find out the following:

1. Where is the federal government located?
2. How is the federal government organized?
3. What does the federal government do for the people of Canada?
4. What symbols does Canada have?
5. (You may want to add some questions of your own.)

Start Thinking about a Project

Ms. Rose told the students that at a later stage they would each be doing a project on Canada. She suggested that they think about making a song, chart, or mobile on what they learned about the federal government and Canada's special symbols. They should each start thinking about the project now and she would give them more information later.

Start Gathering Information

"For now, let's start by gathering information on Canada's federal government. The federal government looks after matters affecting the entire country of Canada," Ms. Rose continued.

"Will we be using non-fiction books to learn about the federal government?" asked Megan.

"Yes. We'll start by reading the information in this book. Then you should look in other non-fiction and reference books in the library, or on the internet."

Record the Best Information

"When you find information that answers your questions, you should record this information in your research notes. Remember not to copy from the books you are using or off the internet. Write the information in your own words."

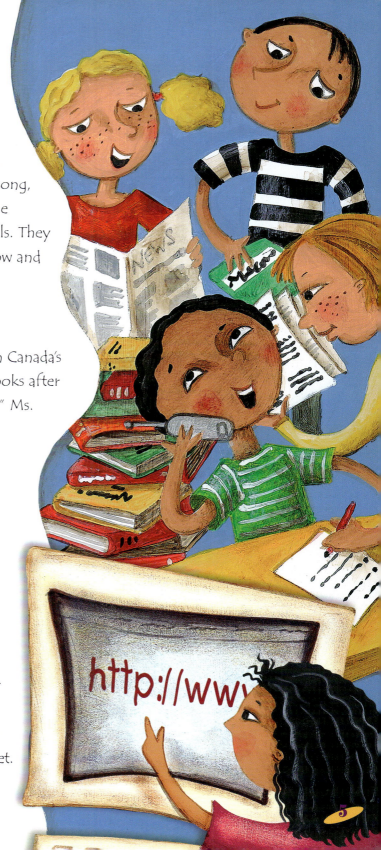

http://www

Canada's Federal Government

Every country in the world is run by a government. The government that looks after matters affecting all of Canada is called the *federal government*. Canada's federal government is located in Ottawa. The leader of Canada's federal government is called a *prime minister*.

The Parliament of Canada

Canada's government is called a *democracy*. Canada's federal parliament is located in Ottawa in an area called *Parliament Hill*. The federal government holds meetings and does its work in these buildings. Most of the important meetings take place in the Centre Block. The diagram on the next page shows how Canada's federal parliament is organized.

Websites
www.parl.gc.ca
http://parliamenthill.gc.ca/text/explorethehill_e.html
www.canadascapital.gc.ca/education

MAP LEGEND
⊛ Capital City
(Federal Government)

0   1000 km

0   500 km

Ottawa

The place where the government of a country, province, or territory is located is called the *capital*. Ottawa is the capital of Canada.

This photograph is of the Parliament Buildings, one of Canada's national symbols. It shows the Centre Block. The Centre Block includes the Peace Tower and library, the House of Commons, the Senate, and a variety of offices.

Organization of Canada's Federal Government

Queen (represented by the Governor General)

Federal Parliament

House of Commons

Cabinet
Prime Minister (PM)
Ministers

Senate
(Appointed)

Members of Parliament (MPs)

Elected by Canadian citizens over the age of 18

Head of Government (PM) and Heads of Departments (Ministers)

Services for the People of Canada
(See page 8.)

Legend

 Her Majesty Queen Elizabeth II is Canada's head of state. The Governor General of Canada is the Queen's representative in Canada.

 Canadians elect people to represent them in the House of Commons. These people are called members of Parliament (or MPs).

 The people in the Senate are chosen by the prime minister and then appointed by the Governor General. These people are called senators.

The people who Canadians elect to represent them meet in the federal parliament to discuss and pass laws. The federal parliament is made up of the Queen (represented by the Governor General), the House of Commons, and the Senate.

Federal Government Services

The government of Canada has many powers and responsibilities. It also provides many services for the people of Canada. This page shows some examples.

Canada's flag

National defence and foreign affairs

Fisheries

Aboriginal people

Trade, commerce, and shipping

National parks

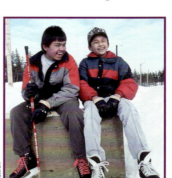

©Canada Post Corporation, 1999. Reproduced with Permission.
Post office

Money and banking

Criminal law

Citizenship and immigration

NO STOPPING AT ANY TIME
ARRÊT INTERDIT EN TOUT TEMPS

Canada's two official languages are French and English.

Health care

Taxation

8

Tools for Learning

Symbols and icons represent (or stand for) ideas.

The maple leaf is a symbol. When you see a red maple leaf on goods in a store, you know they're made in Canada. When you see the Tools for Learning icon (above), you know you'll be learning a new skill. Symbols and icons may be letters, drawings, signs, emblems, characters, or numbers. Non-fiction books often use them.

Layout

When you see the Layout icon, you know you'll be learning about one part of non-fiction book design.

The maple leaf stands for Canada. The stars and stripes stand for the United States. The panda stands for China.

Tilly is the Research Tutor. When you see her, you know you'll be learning about research and the Tools for Learning.

See also Tools for Learning 36.

to do

1. Make T-Notes on pages 6 to 11. (See Tools for Learning 50 for suggestions.)

2. With an adult present, use an internet search engine to find out more about Canada's official symbols. (See Tools for Learning 27 for ideas.)

3. Besides official symbols, there are many other symbols used to represent Canada. Some examples are hockey, the Stanley Cup, Hockey Night in Canada, the Rocky Mountains, grain elevators, Canada geese, moose, polar bears, maple syrup, and beaded mukluks. Choose two to draw.

4. Who is Canada's prime minister?

5. When some Canadians travel outside of Canada, they wear a maple leaf pin. Why?

6. Ask your teacher for Assessment Sheet 1 (Research Step 1, Gathering Information).

Canadian Symbols

The symbols on these two pages represent Canada. Across Canada and throughout the world, they are identified with Canada. Symbols such as these show what's unique about our country. They make us proud to be Canadians.

The crown at the top of Canada's coat of arms represents Her Majesty Queen Elizabeth II, Canada's official head of state.

Bailey, Karen E./National Archives of Canada/C-143716

Canada's coat of arms includes symbols of the peoples that first settled Canada: the French, English, Irish, and Scottish. Canada's motto *A mari usque ad mare* means *From sea even unto sea.*

The maple tree and the maple leaf have been a symbol of Canada since the 1700s.

The maple leaf is one of Canada's most important symbols. The Canadian flag shows the official colours of Canada, red and white. The Maple Leaf became Canada's official flag in 1965.

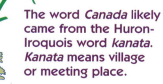

The word *Canada* likely came from the Huron-Iroquois word *kanata*. *Kanata* means village or meeting place.

O Canada!
   Our home and native land!
True patriot love
   in all thy sons command.

With glowing hearts
   we see thee rise,
The True North
   strong and free!

From far and wide,
   O Canada,
      we stand on guard for thee.

God keep our land
   glorious and free!
O Canada,
   we stand on guard for thee.

O Canada,
   we stand on guard for thee.

O Canada is Canada's national anthem. The music to *O Canada* was written by Calixa Lavallée. Other Canadian songs include *God Save the Queen*, *The Maple Leaf Forever*, *Alouette*, and *This Land is Your Land*.

The Dominion of Canada came into being in 1867. Sir John A. Macdonald was Canada's first prime minister.

One symbol of Canada is the beaver, shown here on Canada's five-cent coin.

The Royal Canadian Mounted Police are Canada's national police service.

Research Step 2
Looking at and Organizing Information®

"May I have your attention, please?" asked Tilly as she spoke to the class. "You have been working on Research Step 1, Gathering Information, to collect information on the research topic, *Prepare a project on the government of Canada and the special symbols Canada has.* I would like you to work on the To Do section of this page as part of Research Step 2."

to do

1. a) With a partner, write down or tell each other what things should be done as part of Research Step 2, Looking at and Organizing Information. Check your answers by reading Tools for Learning 4.

    b) Work by yourself or with a partner to carry out Research Step 2.

2. Ask your teacher for Assessment Sheet 2 (Research Step 2, Looking at and Organizing Information).

Research Step 3
Passing on Information®

Tilly pointed to the whiteboard and reminded the students that it was important to follow the **PPSJ**® model when passing on their findings.

Tilly then asked the students to talk about how they were going to share what they had learned about Canada's federal government and the symbols of Canada. After a long discussion, the students decided they would each make a poster. Some students also decided to make up a song about what they had learned.

PPSJ® Model

P = Pick a project that you want to use to share what you've learned. Make plans on when and how you are going to do the project. (See Tools for Learning 70.)

P = Prepare your project. Show it to a friend and ask him or her to suggest ways to make it better. Make changes if they are needed. (See Tools for Learning 71 and 98.)

S = Share your project with your class or your teacher. (See Tools for Learning 99.)

J = Judge your project. Record in your journal what you would do differently next time. What would you do the same? (See Tools for Learning 100.)

Ms. Rose liked all of the students' ideas. She reminded them to be sure they included only information on the research questions they had listed at the beginning of the project. (See page 4.)

The students carefully prepared their projects. They shared them with each other and suggested changes to improve their work.

to do

1. Ask your teacher for an Assessment Sheet on the project you did.

2. Ask your teacher for Assessment Sheet 3 (Research Step 3, Passing on Information).

3. On page 1 of this book, you did a previewing activity (Tools for Learning 1). Did you find the answers to the questions you asked? If you did, write them in your journal now. If you didn't, go back through the book to find the answers. When you find them, write them in your journal.

Glossary

Aboriginal—Canada's first people. Indian (First Nation), Inuit, and Metis are Aboriginal people.

Anthem—a song praising a country. *O Canada* is the national anthem of Canada.

Assessment—a way to help you decide how well you did on a task or skill so that you can improve and do better in the future

Citizenship—one who belongs to a country. A citizen has special rights but also has responsibilities. A person can become a citizen of Canada through birth or by living in Canada for three years, learning English or French, and passing a test on Canada's history and customs.

Democracy—the type of government where the people elect their own leaders. In a democracy citizens have equal rights and basic freedoms.

Dispute—to disagree, argue, or fight over something

Elect—to choose someone by voting

Federal government—a government with national powers. Canada's federal government is located in Ottawa.

Government—the people in a country, province, territory, or community who make and carry out laws, and organize and provide services

Governor General—Her Majesty Queen Elizabeth II's representative in Canada (see also *represent*)

Head of state—the highest or main person in the country. Her Majesty Queen Elizabeth II is Canada's head of state.

House of Commons—part of Canada's federal government. Canadians elect people to represent them in the House of Commons. Laws are made there.

Icon—see *symbol*

Kanata—the source of Canada's name, likely a Huron-Iroquois word meaning *village* or *meeting place*

Law—rules and decisions made by governments for all the people living within a particular area

Legend—the key that lists the information on a map or diagram. It uses lines, arrows, symbols, and colours to explain a map or diagram.

Local government—having to do with the area in which one lives: a city, town, county, or village. In Canada there are hundreds of local governments. Local government in Canada is watched over by the provincial government.

Mobile— a way to display information. There are many ways to make a mobile, but all mobiles consist of pieces of information, balanced and hanging from strings that are attached to something solid.

Motto—a saying about how to do something. For example, a school's motto may be "Help others to do better."

National—having to do with an entire country. Canada's federal government is sometimes called our national government because it is the government for all of Canada.

Parliament—a group of people who make the laws for a country or province

Power—ability; to be in charge, to do things, to make change

Prime minister—the leader (the head) of Canada's federal government

Provincial government—each of the ten provinces in Canada has its own government. The government of each province has different powers than Canada's main government, the federal government.

Represent—to show something or to stand for something. For example, the maple leaf stands for Canada.

Representative—someone chosen to act for or to speak for others

Senate—part of Canada's parliament. Members of the Senate are appointed not elected.

Symbol—a way of representing (showing) an idea; something that stands for something else. Symbols may be letters, drawings, signs, emblems, or numbers. Symbols are also called icons or logos.

Territorial government—a government that is watched over by the federal government. Each territory has its own elected government but these governments do not have the powers that a province has.

Unique—special, one of a kind, different from all others

Picture Credits
The publisher gratefully acknowledges the assistance of the various public institutions, private firms, and individuals who provided materials for use in this book. Every effort has been made to identify and credit all sources. The publisher would appreciate notification of any omissions or errors so that they may be corrected.

Some content this publication © 1999/2000 EyeWire, Inc. All rights reserved.; Copyright © 2004 Hemera Technologies Inc. and its licensors. All rights reserved.; Copyright © Corel Corporation 1995; © Copyright 1998 PhotoDisc, Inc. All rights reserved.; Copyright © 1997 Lampo Communication Inc. All worldwide rights reserved.; © Thinkstock/Getty Images; © Photodisc Collection/Getty Images **page 8 (Aboriginal people image)** © Fred Cattroll; **(National defence image)** Courtesy of the Department of National Defence/Cpl Grant Rivalin; **(Post office image)** © Canada Post Corporation, 1999. Reproduced with Permission.; **(Citizenship image)** Judy Bauer; **(Taxation image)** Canada Customs and Revenue Agency. Reproduced with permission of the Minister of Public Works and Government Services Canada, 2004 **page 10 (left)** Bailey, Karen E./National Archives of Canada/C-143716; **(top right)** CP (John Stillwell) **page 11 (top right)** Glenbow Archives/NA-1375-1; **(bottom right)** RCMP-GRC/RCMP-100410